The Joy of Irish Music

Best-loved songs and folk tunes in easy piano arrang
Selected and arranged by Denes Agay and Frank N

Order No. YK 21793
US International Standard Book Number: 0.8256.8098.0
UK International Standard Book Number: 0.7119.6757.1

Exclusive Distributors:
Music Sales Corporation
257 Park Avenue South, New York, NY 10010 USA
Music Sales Limited
8/9 Frith Street, London W1V 5TZ England
Music Sales Pty. Limited
120 Rothschild Street, Rosebery, Sydney, NSW 2018, Australia

Printed in the United States of America by
Vicks Lithograph and Printing Corporation

Yorktown Music Press, Inc.
New York/London/Sydney

Contents

Barndoor Jig

Traditional

Brennan on the Moor

Traditional

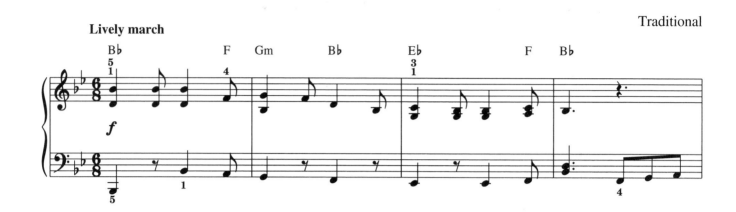

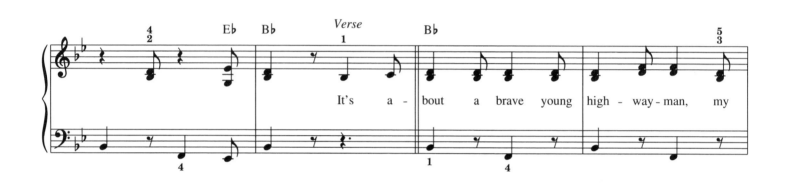

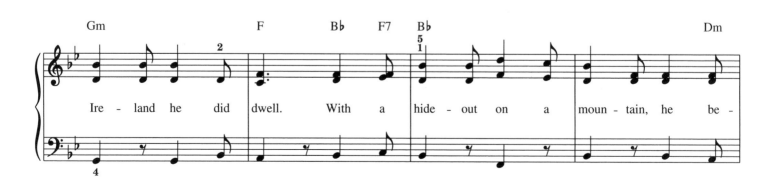

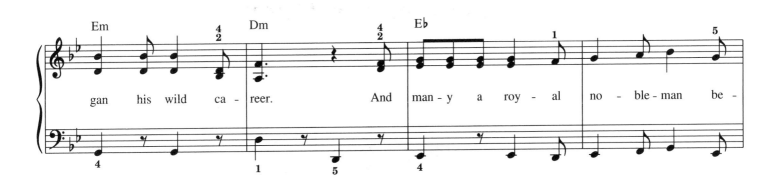

gan his wild ca - reer. And man - y a roy - al no - ble - man be -

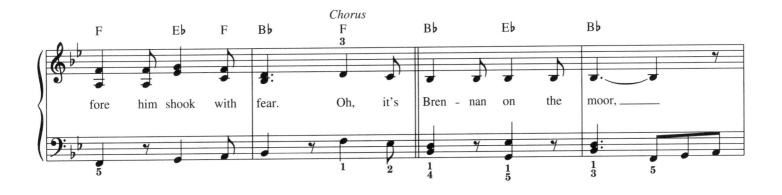

Chorus

fore him shook with fear. Oh, it's Bren - nan on the moor, _____

Bren - nan on the moor, _____ Fear - less, _____ un - daunt - ed was young

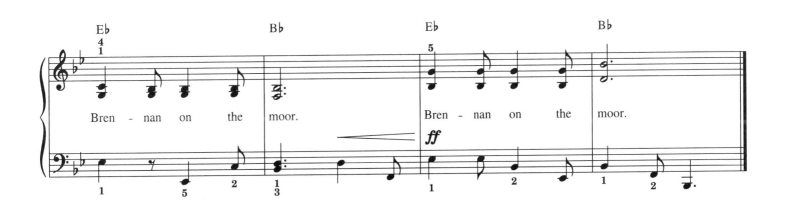

Bren - nan on the moor. Bren - nan on the moor.

Christmas in Ireland

Frank Metis

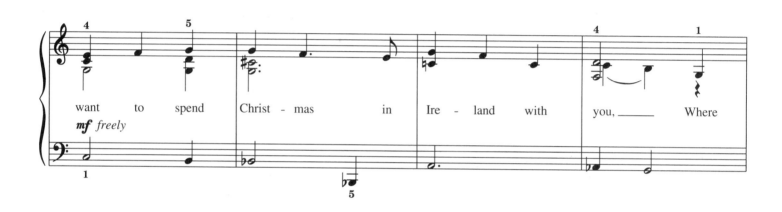

want to spend Christ - mas in Ire - land with you, _____ Where

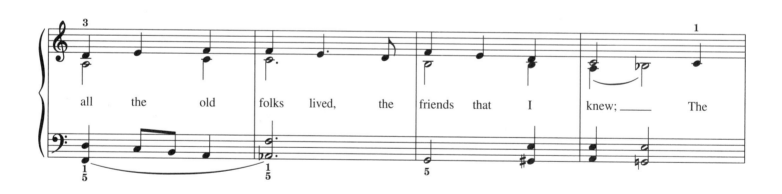

all the old folks lived, the friends that I knew; _____ The

streets that I'd walk, the dreams I would climb, _____ To

wild - wood, _____ I yearn for the roots of my

Er - in tree, Where I grew up, my heart 'll

al - ways be. I need to go back for my

soul to re - new, _____ I want to spend Christ - mas in

ritard.

Ire - land with you.

mp ——— *p*

Garryowen

Traditional

Danny Boy

Londonderry Air

Lyrics by Frederick Edward Weatherly

Freely, with expression

Traditional

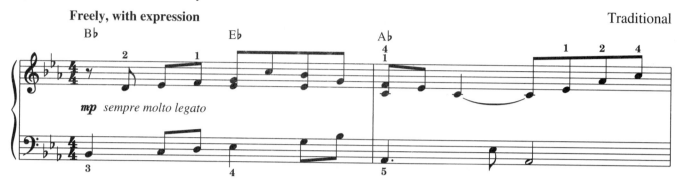

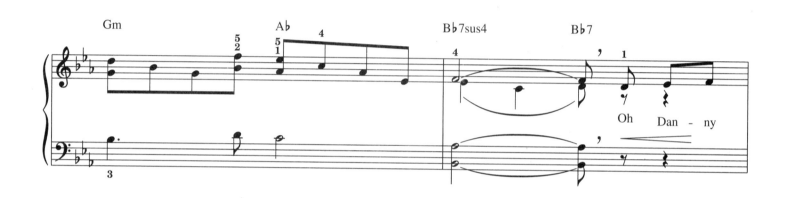

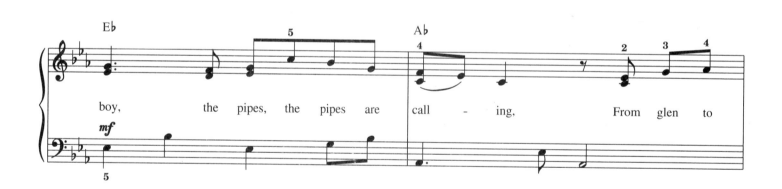

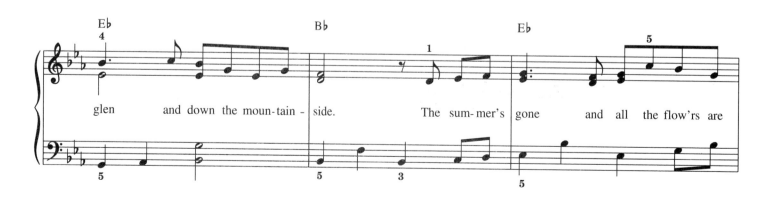

Dear Old Donegal

Traditional

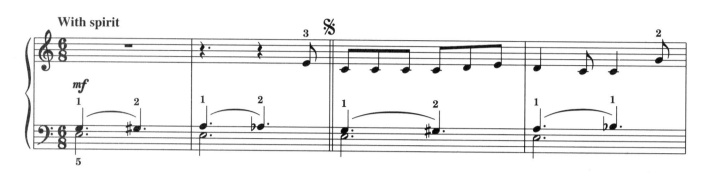

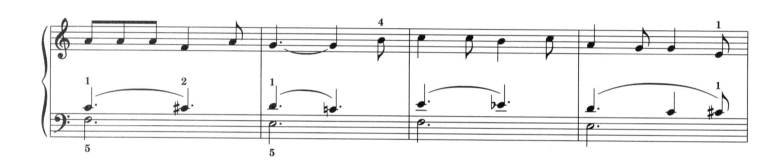

The Emigrant's Voyage to America

Traditional

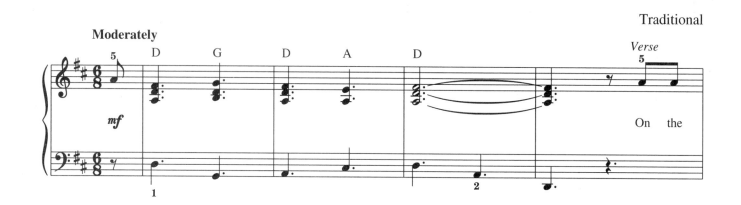

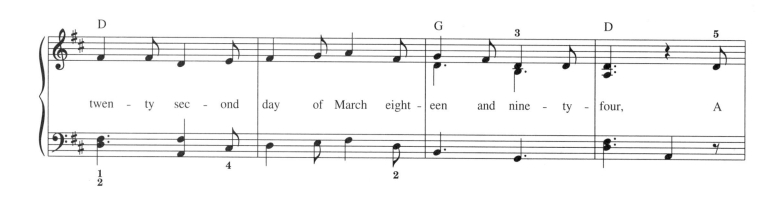

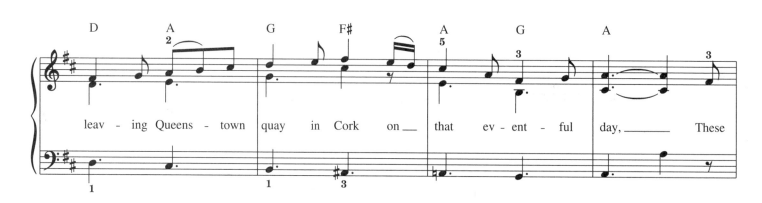

Erin's Green Shore

Traditional

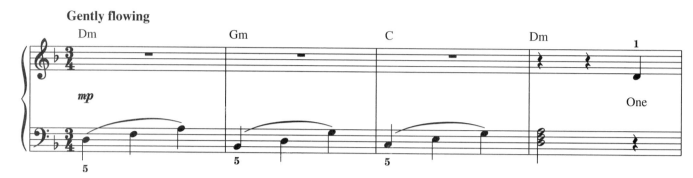

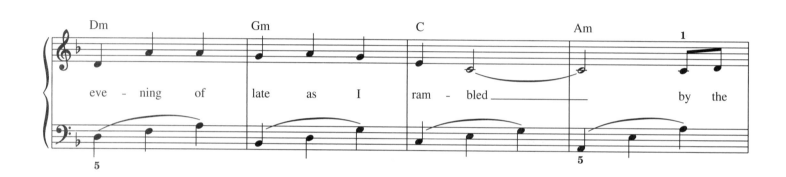

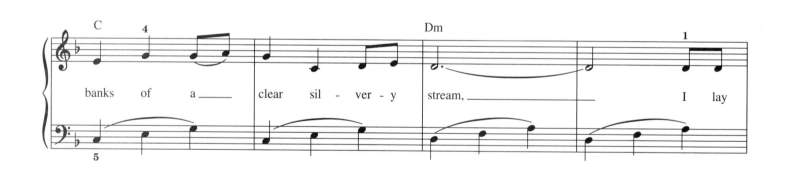

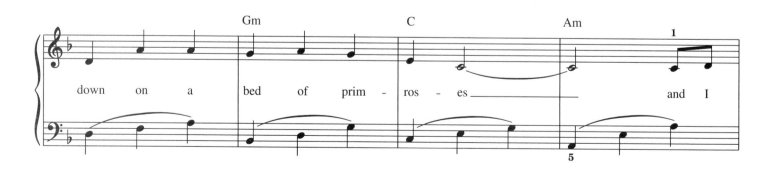

The Foggy, Foggy Dew

Traditional

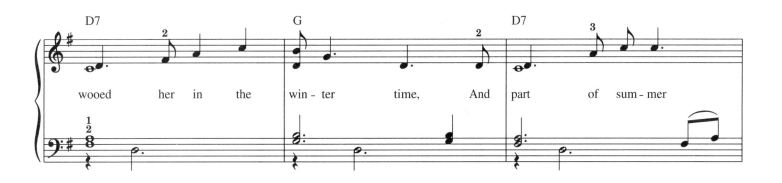

wooed her in the win - ter time, And part of sum - mer

too. And the on - ly, on - ly thing that I

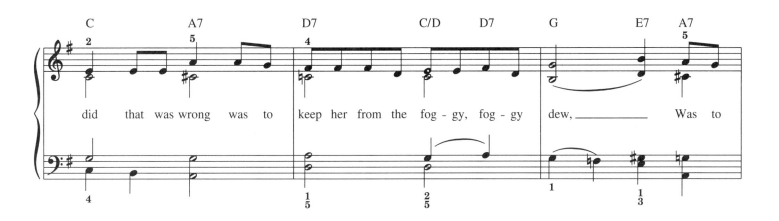

did that was wrong was to keep her from the fog - gy, fog - gy dew, _____ Was to

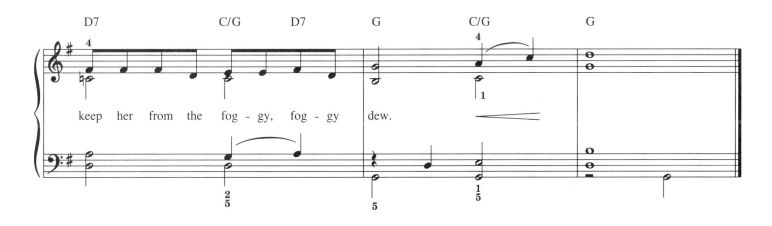

keep her from the fog - gy, fog - gy dew.

Irish March

Frank Metis

Gentleman's Jig

Frank Metis

Lively, with sophisticated reserve

I'll Take You Home Again, Kathleen

Thomas P. Westendorf

The Irish Doc

Frank Metis

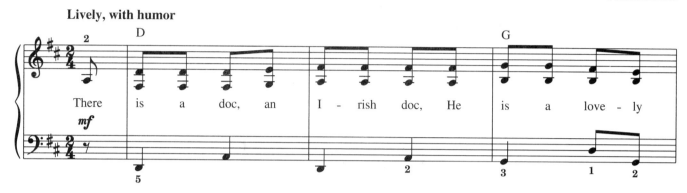

Lively, with humor

There is a doc, an I - rish doc, He is a love - ly

man. To heal the sick, he has a shtick, He'll do the best he

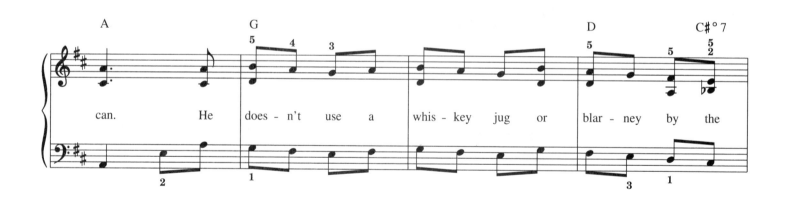

can. He does - n't use a whis - key jug or blar - ney by the

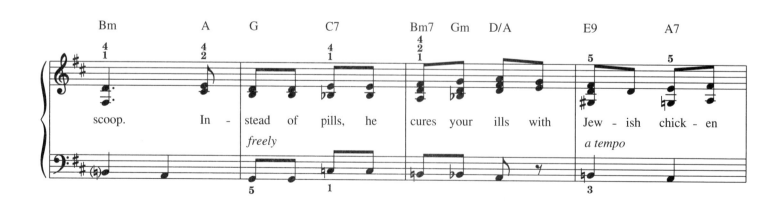

scoop. In - stead of pills, he cures your ills with Jew - ish chick - en

freely   *a tempo*

To Dr. McCarron

An Irish Fantasy

Frank Metis

Freely flowing, not too fast

somewhat slower

rall.

In 6, flowingly, with expression

mf (a tempo)

poco rit.

Irish - Jewish - Viennese - Latin - Africasian Polka

Frank Metis

Irish Pavilion

Based on the old fiddle tune "The Dancingmaster"

Frank Metis

Very freely

Lively, with spirit

The Irish Rover

Traditional

beaut - i - ful craft, she was rigged fore and aft, And

Lord, how the trade winds drove _____ her, _____ As she

stood to the blast, she had twen - ty - three masts, And we

called her the Ir - ish Rov - er.

No chord

An Irish Prayer

Frank Metis

The Last Rose of Summer

Traditional

The Kerry Dance

Traditional

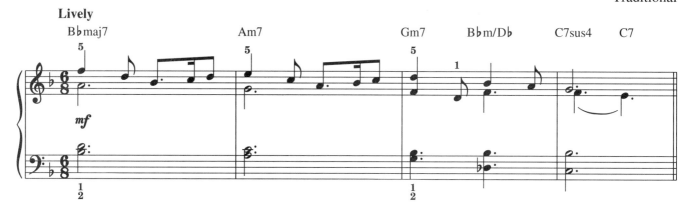

McNamara's Band

Traditional

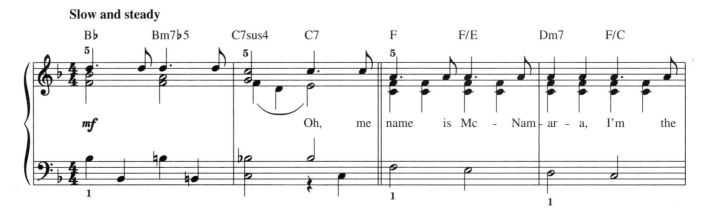

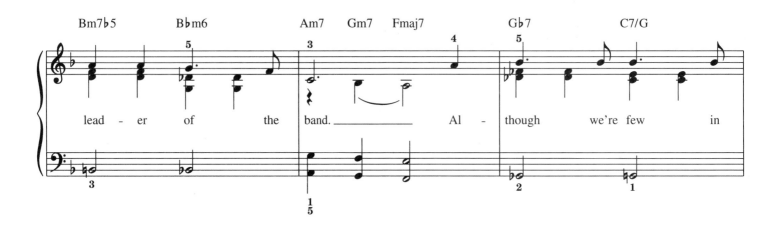

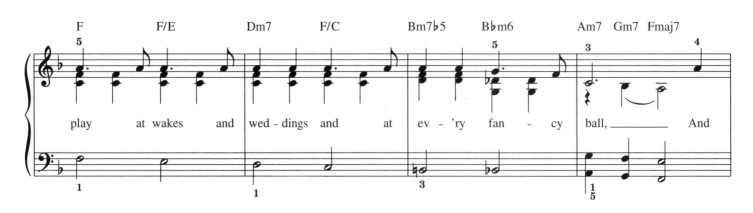

My Beautiful Shannon

Lyrics by Michael J. Hogan

Traditional

A Visit to Ireland

Jig

Traditional

My Wild Irish Rose

Chauncey Olcott

Flowingly, with expression

mf sempre legato

My

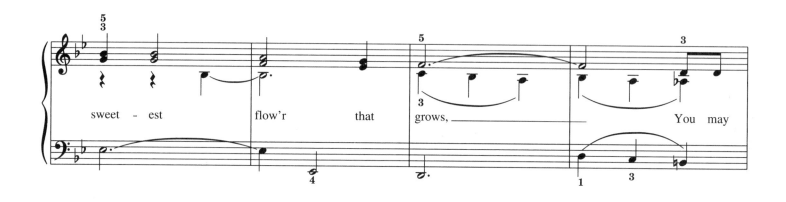

wild   I – rish   Rose, _____   The

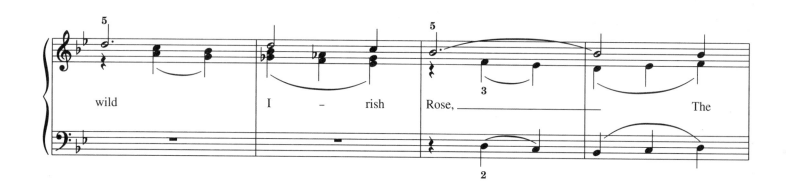

sweet - est   flow'r   that   grows, _____   You may

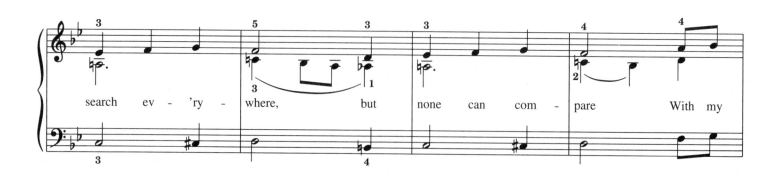

search   ev - 'ry -   where,   but   none   can   com - pare   With my

St. Patrick's Day in the Morning

Traditional

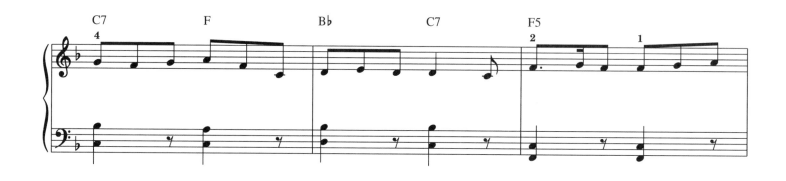

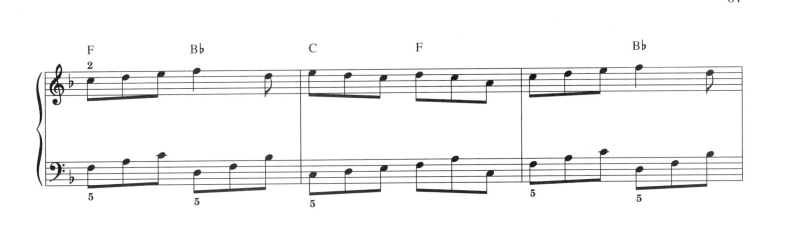

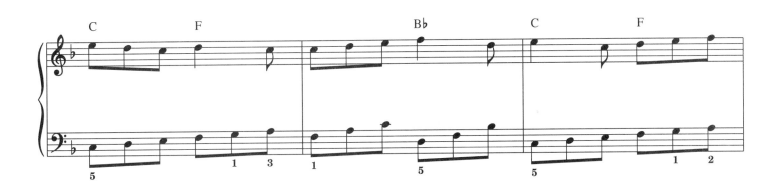

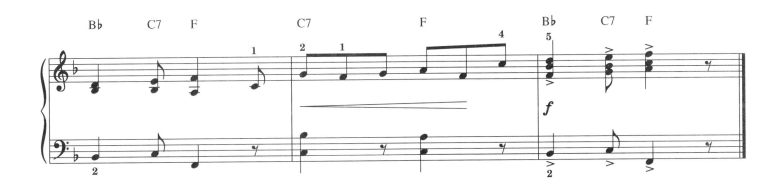

Stack of Barley
Reel

Traditional

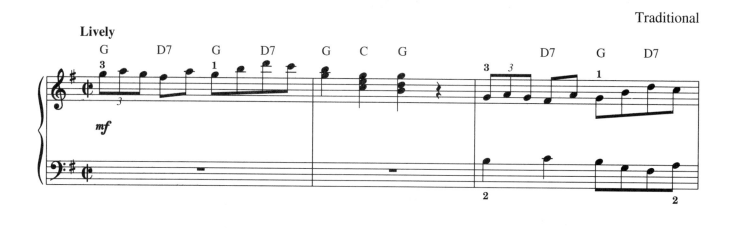

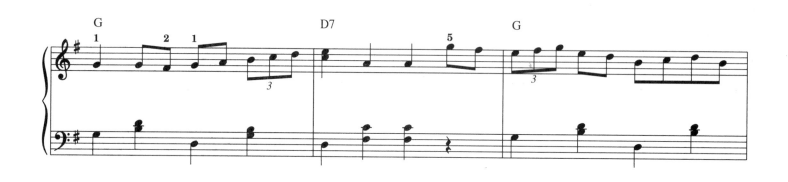

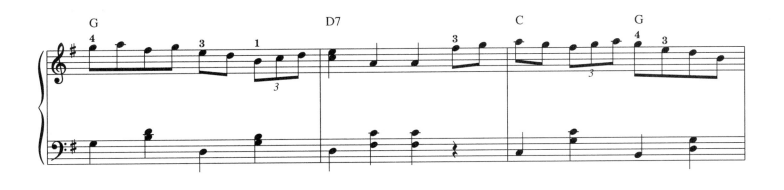

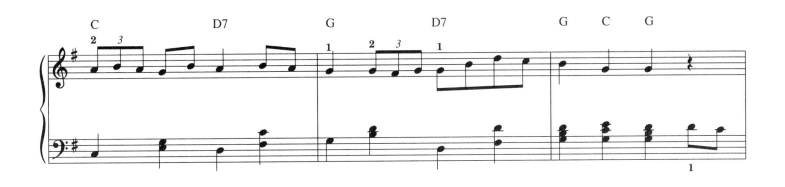

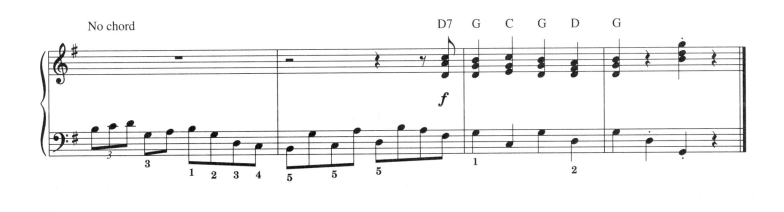

A Little Bit of Heaven
Sure, They Call It Ireland

Lyrics by Keirn Brennan

Music by Ernest R. Ball

Sweet Molly Malone

Traditional

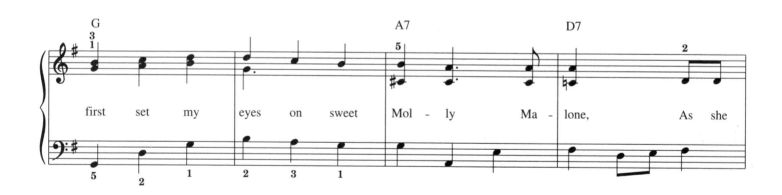

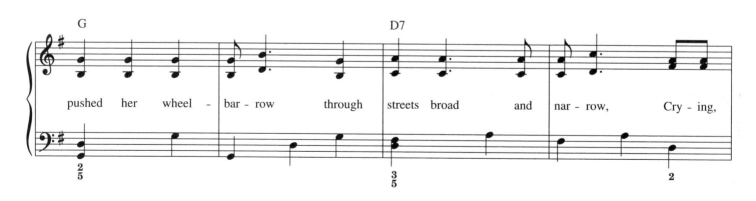

63

Swingin' Seafood

Cockles and Mussels

Adapted from the Traditional

Moderate swing (with a ♩.♪ feel)

(Right hand with a light touch)

Peg o' My Heart

Lyrics by Alfred Bryan

Music by Fred Fisher

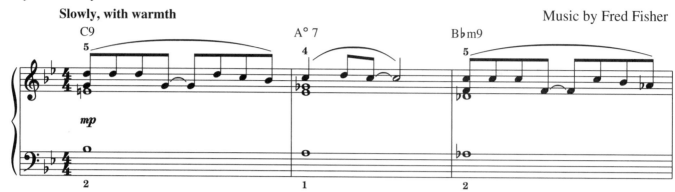

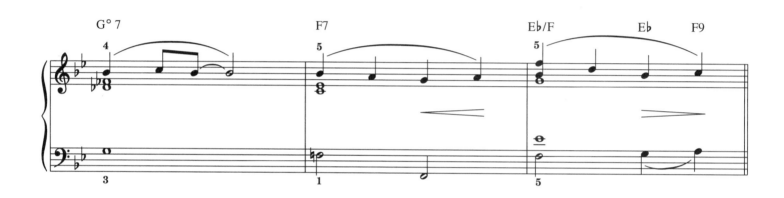

Peg o' my heart,_____ I love you, We'll nev - er part,_____

_____ I love you, Dear lit - tle girl,___ Sweet lit - tle girl,___

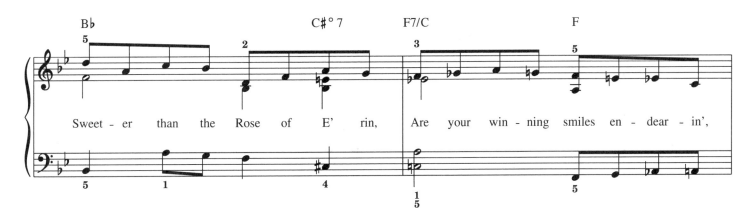

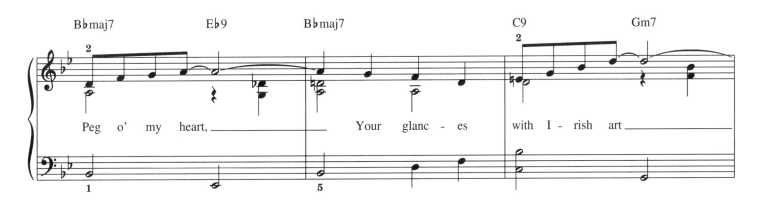

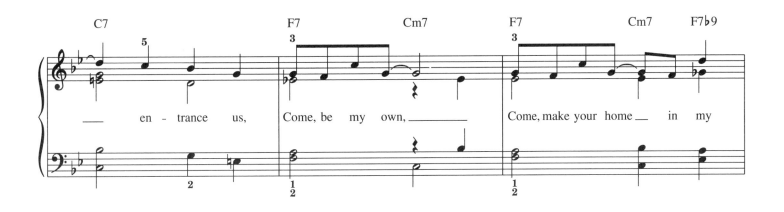

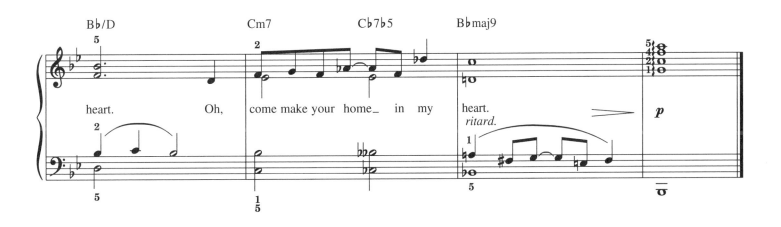

To Ireland

A Toast

Frank Metis

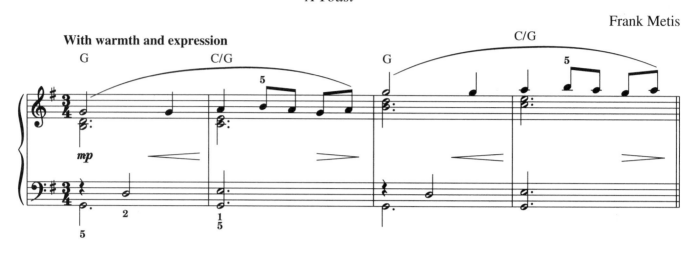

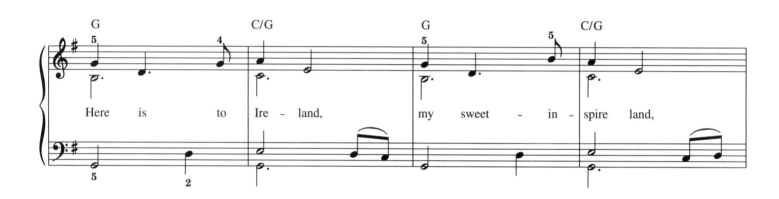

Here is to Ire - land, my sweet - in - spire land,

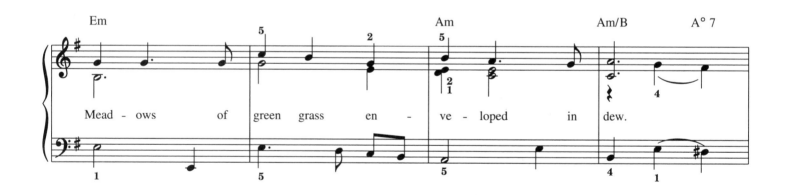

Mead - ows of green grass en - ve - loped in dew.

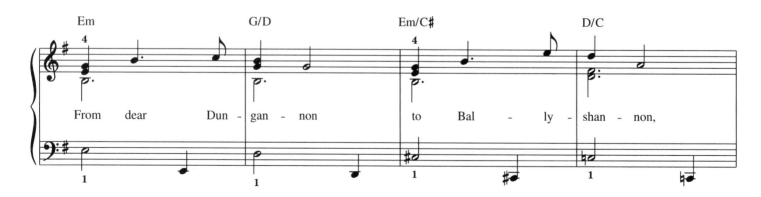

From dear Dun - gan - non to Bal - ly - shan - non,

Too-Ra-Loo-Ra-Loo-Ral
(That's an Irish Lullaby)

J. R. Shannon

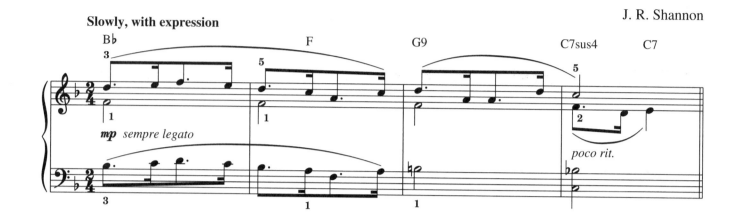

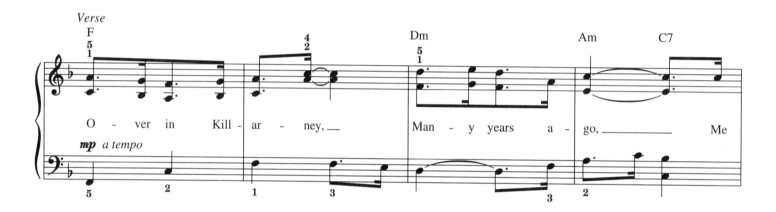

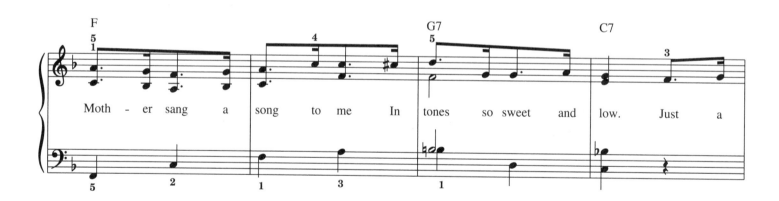

The Wearing of the Green

W. E. Hudson (1841)

When Irish Eyes Are Smiling

Lyrics by Chauncey Olcott and George Graff, Jr.

Music by Ernest R. Ball

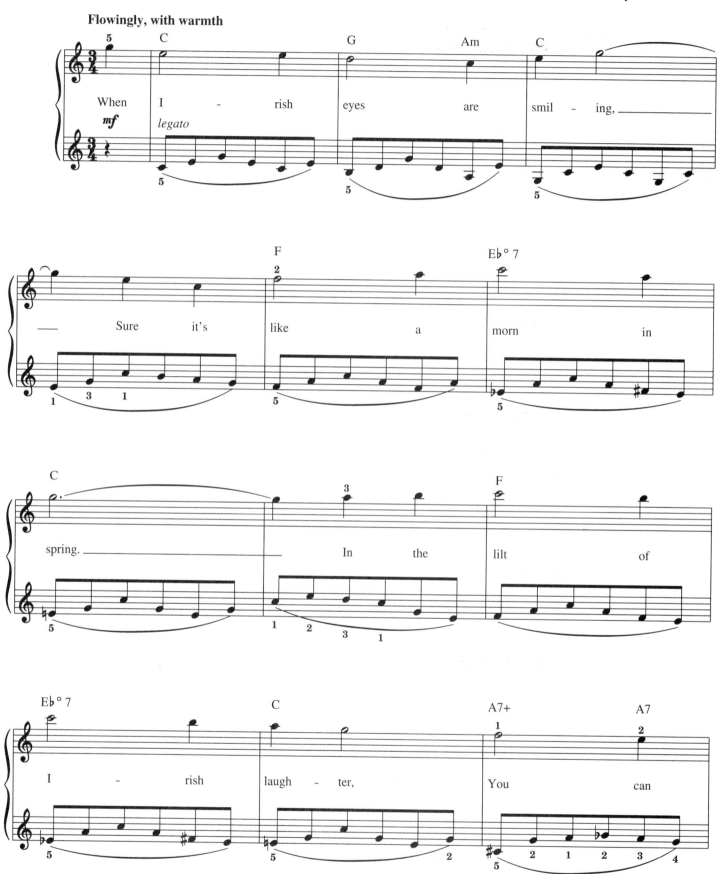

The Wild Rover

Traditional

With spirit

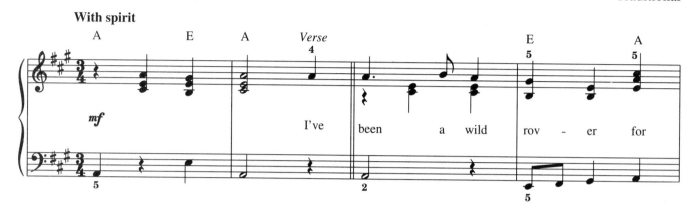

I've been a wild rov - er for

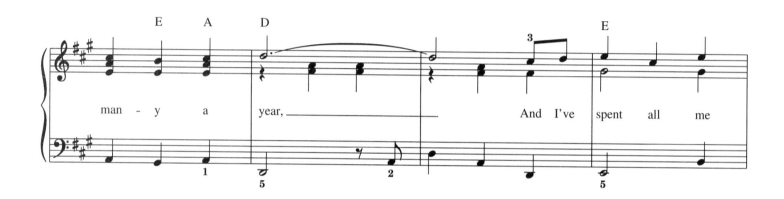

man - y a year, _____ And I've spent all me

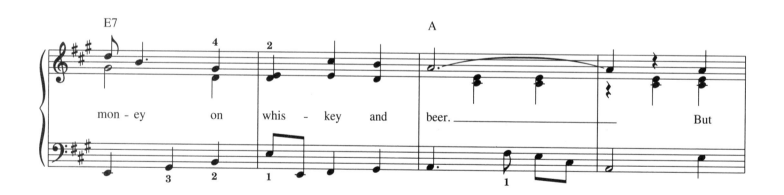

mon - ey on whis - key and beer. _____ But

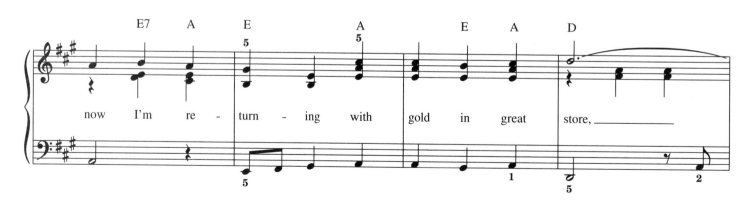

now I'm re - turn - ing with gold in great store, _____

The Wily Old Bachelor

Traditional Fiddle Tune

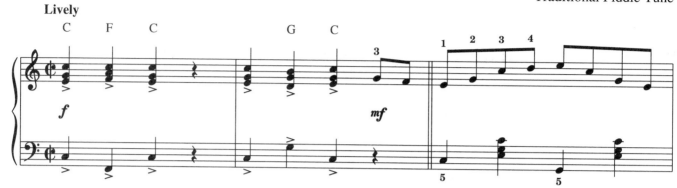

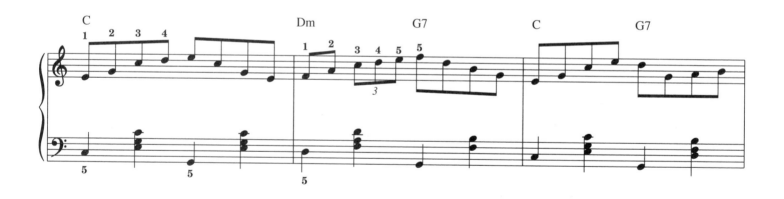

The Washerwoman

Traditional

COLLEGE LONDON

Guitar Grade 3

Pieces & Exercises
for Trinity College London examinations

2010-2015

Published by:
Trinity College London
89 Albert Embankment
London SE1 7TP UK

T +44 (0)20 7820 6100
F +44 (0)20 7820 6161
E music@trinitycollege.co.uk
www.trinitycollege.co.uk

Music processed by Artemis Music Ltd.
Printed in England by Halstan & Co. Ltd, Amersham, Bucks.

Menuet

from *Resumen de acompañar la parte con la guitarra*

Santiago de Murcia
(*c.* 1673-1739)

- use metronome
- gentle accent on 1st beat
- play loud

3

Minuet

op. 21 no. 12

Matteo Carcassi
(1792-1853)

Ländler

op. 9 no. 4

Johann Kaspar Mertz
(1806-1856)

Sakura

arr. Lee Sollory

Traditional Japanese

(*1*) Slowly, bending the string slightly out of tune.

Carratera resbaladiza

Cees Hartog
(born 1949)

Valse noble

from *Eight Short Pieces for Solo Guitar*

Peter Berlind Carlson
(born 1956)

Walking

from *8 Discernments*

Andrew York
(born 1958)

Banjo Bill

Gary Ryan
(born 1969)

Station to Station

Lee Sollory
(born 1959)

Technical Suite (Exercises)

Candidates choosing Option ii) Technical Suite in the Technical Work section of the examination must prepare the following exercises.

1. Jiggery Pokery (scales)

To be prepared *apoyando* or *tirando* at candidate's choice.*

2. Thurdles (broken chords)

To be prepared *tirando*.

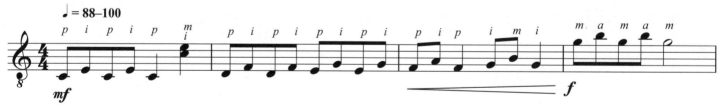

* *apoyando* = rest stroke; *tirando* = free stroke.

3. Au lait (half barré)

4. Passagio (arpeggios)